MW00881151

This journal belongs to:

Hold up your head!
You were not made for failure,
you were made for victory.

Go forward with a joyful confidence.

George Eliot

Dear Reader,

Thanks for purchasing our book.

We feel grateful to serve you with our carefully created:

The 365 Self-Discovery Journal

& Hope you enjoy, learn and find what you're looking for.

All the best,

21 Exercises

As a little thank you note,
we've three Free Personal-Growth exercises waiting for you.

Simply send an email to to exercises21@yahoo.com
Title the email "365 Journal"

And we will send you Three Personal Development Hacks for FREE.

The 365 Self-Discovery Journal

Copyright © 2018- 21 Exercises

All rights reserved.
No part of this publication may be reproduced, distributed, or transmitted in any form or by any means, including photocopying, recording, or other electronic or mechanical methods, without the prior written permission of the publisher, except in the case of brief quotations embodied in critical reviews and certain other noncommercial uses permitted by copyright law. For permission requests, write to the publisher.

Disclaimer
This book is not intended to be a substitute for medical advice or treatment. Any person with a condition requiring medical attention should consult a qualified medical practitioner or suitable therapist.
The information provided in this book is stated to be truthful and consistent, in that any liability, in terms of inattention or otherwise, by any usage or abuse of any policies, processes, or directions contained within is the solitary and utter responsibility of the recipient reader. Under no circumstances will any legal responsibility or blame be held against the publisher for any reparation, damages, or monetary loss due to the information herein, either directly or indirectly.

The
365 Self-Discovery Journal

One Year Of Reflection, Development & Happiness

Created by:

21 Exercises

True Potential Project

2018

Introduction

Who in the world am I? Ah, that's the great puzzle.

Lewis Carroll, *Alice in Wonderland*

There is no one who knows you better yourself. But that knowledge is often hidden behind thick clouds of social conditioning, suppressed feelings and old beliefs. Most of the time, more external information isn't *the* solution for actual self-discovery. The truth is within. Your answers are already there. So we did not create yet another general self-help book. We've created an insightful, practical and inspiring self-discovery journal. Because it isn't our information that is gold, it is your own. Thus this book is created for those who dare to take the most courageous road of all: the road within. An inward journey.

For one year this book will supply you with original, challenging and impressing questions to guide you on this journey. All combined with quotes and poems from the greatest minds of all-time. Furthermore, there will be small weekly and monthly challenges to help you improve your life and expand your comfort zone one small step at a time. The journal will cover every area of your life, from health, to finances, to your career to improving your love life. It also focuses on gratefulness and acknowledging your own strengths and talents. Is it intimidating and time consuming? No. We wanted it to make it as easy as possible to follow through on using this journal every day. With so much as five minutes per day you will be able to finish the vast majority of the work in the journal.

Is that all? Almost. Most importantly, this journal will give you the tools to uncover what is hidden beneath the surface. To uncover what is holding you back in life. To shine light on old and uncomfortable beliefs, thoughts and desires that live within you. In your shadow self. A part of yourself that has a big subconscious impact in your daily life.

With this journal we are giving you the tools to become whole again. To live the life you want, and not a life that is based on old, limited beliefs from your childhood and distracting thoughts from your shadow self. These uncovering questions are specifically placed all throughout the journal. This way it never will be too intimidating but the effect on your life will be amazing.

All in all this is an easy to use daily journal. And it will surely inspire you, to have astonishing insights to change your life for the better, within as much as five minutes a day.

How To Use This Journal

Every page of this book contains two days, posing a new question or short challenge for each day. There is enough space on each page to answer the question / make a plan for the challenge, and do more journaling. Do you need more journaling space? At the end of this book, we added a couple of more blank pages.

We recommend setting a particular time each day for your journaling exercises. For example, during your morning routine or before going to bed. By choosing a particular time each day, you could integrate journaling as a short, simple and easy to follow habit in your life.

Throughout this book, you're going to find similar questions, mainly concerning the topics of gratefulness and your own strengths. We've specifically done this to really bring these topics, which we often tend to forget, into the spotlight.

"The unthankful heart discovers no mercies; but the thankful heart will find, in every hour, some heavenly blessings."
Henry Ward Beecher

Day 1 - What has made your childhood worthwhile?

_____
_____
_____
_____
_____
_____
_____
_____
_____
_____
_____

Day 2 - What would happen if you would treat the actions you fear as an experiment?

_____
_____
_____
_____
_____
_____
_____
_____
_____
_____
_____

"Those who know, do. Those that understand, teach."
Aristotle

Day 3 - What could other people learn from you?

_____
_____
_____
_____
_____
_____
_____
_____
_____
_____
_____

Day 4 - For which pending decision you could use ten percent
more courage?

_____
_____
_____
_____
_____
_____
_____
_____
_____
_____
_____
_____
_____

"A path is made by walking on it."
Zhuang Zhou

Day 5 - Name at least five things you find physically attractive about yourself.

_____

_____

_____

_____

_____

_____

_____

_____

_____

_____

Day 6 - What lessons did you learn last week?

_____

_____

_____

_____

_____

_____

_____

_____

_____

_____

_____

> "I am not afraid of storms,
> for I am learning how to sail my ship."
> Louisa May Alcott

Day 7 - What question(s) always make you feel uncomfortable?

_____
_____
_____
_____
_____
_____
_____
_____
_____
_____
_____

Day 8 - *Comfort zone +.*
What is one tiny thing you could do this week to expand your comfort zone? Write down when and how you are going to do it and put it on your calendar.

(Examples could be asking an attractive stranger for the time, saying no, cooking something new, watching a movie that you would normally skip)

_____
_____
_____
_____
_____
_____
_____
_____

"Tears came, because I understood that the past wasn't just the past.
That those moments weren't just a memory.
They were a promise that life was worthwhile."
Joanne Edmund

Day 9 - What makes life worthwhile for you?

_____
_____
_____
_____
_____
_____
_____
_____
_____
_____
_____

Day 10 - Name ten positive character traits about yourself.

_____
_____
_____
_____
_____
_____
_____
_____
_____
_____
_____

"Hide not your talents, they for use were made,
What's a sundial in the shade?"
Benjamin Franklin

Day 11- What are three things you could do this month
to improve your finances?

_____

_____

_____

_____

_____

_____

_____

_____

_____

Day 12- Which people you spend time with
actually have a negative influence on your life?

_____

_____

_____

_____

_____

_____

_____

_____

_____

_____

"What is that you express in your eyes?
It seems to me more than all the print I have read in my life."
Walt Whitman

Day 13- What trip have you always wanted to make?
Come up with at least three possibilities to make this trip happen.

_____
_____
_____
_____
_____
_____
_____
_____
_____
_____
_____
_____

Day 14 - What positive things would people say behind your back?

_____
_____
_____
_____
_____
_____
_____
_____
_____
_____
_____
_____

"No one is useless in this world
who lightens the burdens of another."
Charles Dickens

Day 15 - How has the media influenced your view on the world?

_____

_____

_____

_____

_____

_____

_____

_____

_____

_____

Day 16 - Which important people in your life could need a little more attention?

_____

_____

_____

_____

_____

_____

_____

_____

_____

_____

_____

_____

"The best revenge is not to be like your enemy."
Marcus Aurelius, *Meditations*

Day 17 - Do you see sex more as an emotional connection or a physical connection? Why?

_____

_____

_____

_____

_____

_____

_____

_____

_____

_____

_____

Day 18 - What could make other people angry about you?

_____

_____

_____

_____

_____

_____

_____

_____

_____

_____

_____

"The best portion of a good man's life:
his little, nameless unremembered acts of kindness and love."
William Wordsworth

Day 19 - Are you still blaming people for things that happened
to you recently?

_____
_____
_____
_____
_____
_____
_____
_____
_____
_____
_____

Day 20 - Write down 12 things for which you are grateful.

_____
_____
_____
_____
_____
_____
_____
_____
_____
_____
_____
_____

"Be thine own palace,
or the world's thy jail."
John Donne

Day 21 - What is the one thing you could do this month to improve your health?

_____
_____
_____
_____
_____
_____
_____
_____
_____
_____

Day 22 - Describe the pattern of when you are procrastinating.

_____
_____
_____
_____
_____
_____
_____
_____
_____
_____
_____
_____

"Never put off till tomorrow what may be done
day after tomorrow just as well."
Mark Twain

Day 23 - What are three things you could do to stop the pattern
of procrastination?

_____

_____

_____

_____

_____

_____

_____

_____

_____

_____

Day 24 - Where in your life are you too hard on yourself?

_____

_____

_____

_____

_____

_____

_____

_____

_____

_____

"Forever is composed of nows."
Emily Dickinson

Day 25 - What do you consider cheating or being unfaithful in a relationship? Why?

_____

_____

_____

_____

_____

_____

_____

_____

_____

_____

_____

Day 26 - Name ten things that make you happy.

_____

_____

_____

_____

_____

_____

_____

_____

_____

_____

_____

_____

"Come friends, it's not too late to seek a newer world."
Alfred Lord Tennyson

Day 27 - Take a look at your *happy list* of yesterday.
How could you integrate more happiness in your life?
Name at least three specific things and how you are going to do it.

Day 28 - What makes you feel sad?

> "In character, in manner, in style, in all the things,
> the supreme excellence is simplicity."
> *Henry Wadsworth Longfellow*

Day 29 - How would you describe your own sadness?

_____
_____
_____
_____
_____
_____
_____
_____
_____
_____
_____

Day 30 - *Monthly challenge*
What is the one thing you could do this month to improve your health?
Write down how you are going to hold yourself accountable.

_____
_____
_____
_____
_____
_____
_____
_____
_____
_____

"If we had no winter, the spring would not be so pleasant:
if we did not sometimes taste of adversity,
prosperity would not be so welcome."

Anne Bradstreet

Day 31 - To what movie character do you relate the most and why?
(For example, *the hero of the movie, femme fatale, destructive artist,
James Bond, Bridget Jones)*

Day 32 - What is positive about the movie character you relate to the
most? And what is negative about it?

"Let us be grateful to the people who make us happy;
they are the charming gardeners who make our souls blossom."
Marcel Proust

Day 33- Where in your life do you act exactly like your favorite movie character? Does it help you?

_____

_____

_____

_____

_____

_____

_____

_____

_____

_____

Day 34 - How does the way you parents loved each other affect your love life nowadays?

_____

_____

_____

_____

_____

_____

_____

_____

_____

_____

If there's not too much sun nor too much cloud,
And the warm wind is neither still nor loud,
Perhaps my secret I may say,
Or you may guess.
Christina Rossetti

Day 35 - Name at least seven moments in your life that made you feel uncomfortable.

_____

_____

_____

_____

_____

_____

_____

_____

_____

_____

Day 36 - Look at your list of yesterday. Is there a common theme in situations that make you feel uncomfortable?

_____

_____

_____

_____

_____

_____

_____

_____

_____

_____

_____

"One ought, every day at least, to hear a little song, read a good poem, see a fine picture, and, if it were possible, to speak a few reasonable words."

Johann Wolfgang von Goethe

Day 37 - What would you want other people to know about you?

_____

_____

_____

_____

_____

_____

_____

_____

_____

_____

_____

Day 38 - Name at least ten things that make you a great person.

_____

_____

_____

_____

_____

_____

_____

_____

_____

_____

_____

"What is now proved was once only imagined."
William Blake

Day 39 - Write down ten things why you think *you are not good enough.*

_____

_____

_____

_____

_____

_____

_____

_____

_____

_____

_____

Day 40 - Look at your list of yesterday. How would your life be different if you accept these things as part of who you are?

_____

_____

_____

_____

_____

_____

_____

_____

_____

_____

_____

"But the cloud never comes in that quarter of the horizon
from which we watch for it."
Elizabeth Gaskell

Day 41 - What is the one thing you could do today,
to live a better tomorrow?

_____
_____
_____
_____
_____
_____
_____
_____
_____
_____

Day 42 - Name at least three experiences that made you feel great
about yourself.

_____
_____
_____
_____
_____
_____
_____
_____
_____
_____

"What I think I've been able to do well over the years is play with pain, play with problems, play in all sorts of conditions."
Roger Federer

Day 43 - How do you march on when life gets difficult?

_____
_____
_____
_____
_____
_____
_____
_____
_____
_____
_____

Day 44 - What are the core values you live by?Name at least three.

_____
_____
_____
_____
_____
_____
_____
_____
_____
_____
_____
_____

"He who is best prepared can best serve his moment of inspiration."
Samuel Taylor Coleridge

Day 45 - What is the one thing you could do this week to improve your personal relationships?

_____

_____

_____

_____

_____

_____

_____

_____

_____

_____

Day 46 - If, because of a medical condition, you could only work 8 hours per week, what would you do?

_____

_____

_____

_____

_____

_____

_____

_____

_____

_____

"Choose love not in the shallows but in the deep."
Christina Rossetti

Day 47 - List at least five things you've always wanted to do.

_____

_____

_____

_____

_____

_____

_____

_____

_____

_____

_____

Day 48 - Take a look at your list of yesterday. Pick one of your dreams
and describe how you could make it happen within six months.

_____

_____

_____

_____

_____

_____

_____

_____

_____

_____

_____

"There's a place in the soul where you've never been wounded."
Meister Eckhart

Day 49 - We will continue where we started yesterday. List down all the reasons that are stopping you to go for that particular dream. Are these reasons worth it to make you stop chasing your dream?

_____

_____

_____

_____

_____

_____

_____

_____

_____

_____

Day 50 - What is the one thing you could do this week to improve your love life?

_____

_____

_____

_____

_____

_____

_____

_____

_____

_____

_____

"Life is not a having and a getting, but a being and a becoming."
Matthew Arnold

Day 51 - Which emotion do you find most difficult to deal with and why?

_____
_____
_____
_____
_____
_____
_____
_____
_____
_____

Day 52 - Imagine one year from now:
what would you regret that you are postponing now?

_____
_____
_____
_____
_____
_____
_____
_____
_____
_____

"Kind words can be short and easy to speak,
but their echoes are truly endless."
Mother Teresa

Day 53 - *Exercise.*
Stand or sit down in front of a mirror for five minutes.
What did you notice and what thoughts came up?

_____

_____

_____

_____

_____

_____

_____

_____

_____

Day 54 - What is one thing you could do this week to be more kind
to the people around you?

_____

_____

_____

_____

_____

_____

_____

_____

_____

_____

"You may delay, but time will not."
Benjamin Franklin

Day 55 - What area of your life are you neglecting and why?

_____

_____

_____

_____

_____

_____

_____

_____

_____

_____

_____

_____

Day 56 - How did you overcome failure in the past? Write down at least one specific failure and what you did to overcome it.

_____

_____

_____

_____

_____

_____

_____

_____

_____

_____

_____

_____

"I'm not strange, weird, off, nor crazy,
my reality is just different from yours."
Lewis Carroll

Day 57 - *Declutter week.*
For this week try every day to clean up or give away stuff you don't
need. For example: clothes, DVDs, magazines, books, accessories.
For now, write down at least three items you don't need.

_____

_____

_____

_____

_____

_____

_____

_____

_____

_____

Day 58 - Write down at least seven things you could do to
reduce stress.

_____

_____

_____

_____

_____

_____

_____

_____

_____

_____

"Better be wise by the misfortunes of others than by your own."
Aesop

Day 59 - How is the way you were raised helping you today?

_____
_____
_____
_____
_____
_____
_____
_____
_____
_____

Day 60 - How is the way you were raised holding you back today?

_____
_____
_____
_____
_____
_____
_____
_____
_____
_____
_____
_____

"When we are no longer able to change a situation,
we are challenged to change ourselves."

Viktor E. Frankl, *Man's Search for Meaning*

Day 61 - Is it time to let go of some old beliefs and old values?
Which ones and why?

_____

_____

_____

_____

_____

_____

_____

_____

_____

Day 62 - What could you do to get yourself motivated? Write down at
least three things.

_____

_____

_____

_____

_____

_____

_____

_____

_____

_____

"In all chaos there is a cosmos, in all disorder a secret order."
Carl Gustav Jung

Day 63 - What past experience would you want to relive? Why?

Day 64 - Is what you do today truly what you want to do?

"It is a narrow mind
which cannot look at a subject from various points of view."
George Eliot

Day 65 - Write down at least five of your accomplishments that make you special.

_____

_____

_____

_____

_____

_____

_____

_____

_____

_____

Day 66 - What is an easier method you could use to achieve your goals? Pick one goal you are struggling with to achieve now for quite some time.

_____

_____

_____

_____

_____

_____

_____

_____

_____

_____

"Resolve to be thyself;
and know, that he who finds himself, loses his misery."
Matthew Arnold

Day 67 - What do you miss the most about your teenage years?

_____
_____
_____
_____
_____
_____
_____
_____
_____

Day 68 - What makes you upset?

_____
_____
_____
_____
_____
_____
_____
_____
_____
_____
_____
_____

"The fool doth think he is wise,
but the wise man knows himself to be a fool."
William Shakespeare, As You Like It

Day 69 -Are you an introvert or an extrovert?
How does that manifest in your daily life?

_____
_____
_____
_____
_____
_____
_____
_____
_____

Day 70 - Take a look at your answers from yesterday.
What are the pros of being an introvert/extrovert?

_____
_____
_____
_____
_____
_____
_____
_____
_____
_____

"Always laugh when you can, it is cheap medicine."
Lord Byron

Day 71 - What are the cons of being an introvert/extrovert?
How could you deal with this?

Day 72 - *Comfort zone ++++.*
What is one tiny thing you could do this week to expand your comfort
zone? Write down when and how you are going to do it and put it on
your calendar.

"Generosity without delicacy, like wit without judgement, generally gives as much pain as pleasure."
Frances Burney

Day 73 - What are you willing to do for love?

_____

_____

_____

_____

_____

_____

_____

_____

_____

_____

_____

Day 74 - If you could change one thing about your past, what would it be and why?

_____

_____

_____

_____

_____

_____

_____

_____

_____

_____

_____

"We must find time to stop and thank the people
who make a difference in our lives."
John F. Kennedy

Day 75 -What made you grateful last week?

Day 76 -Which childhood memories make you still feel joyful?

"If the only prayer you said was thank you,
that would be enough."
Meister Eckhart

Day 77 -What about your childhood is still hurting you today?

_____

_____

_____

_____

_____

_____

_____

_____

_____

_____

Day 78 -Look at your answer from yesterday. Try to come up with three
ways how you could deal with this past experience.

_____

_____

_____

_____

_____

_____

_____

_____

_____

_____

_____

"Set wide the window.
Let me drink the day."
Edith Wharton

Day 79 -If you would bring ten percent more awareness to your
deepest needs, what would happen?

_____

_____

_____

_____

_____

_____

_____

_____

_____

_____

_____

Day 80 -If you would bring ten percent more awareness to your
deepest desires, what would happen?

_____

_____

_____

_____

_____

_____

_____

_____

_____

_____

_____

"Anger is the ultimate destroyer of your own peace of mind"
Dalai Lama

Day 81 - If you would bring ten percent more awareness to your deepest insecurities, what would happen?

_____

_____

_____

_____

_____

_____

_____

_____

_____

_____

Day 82 - What are better ways to deal with your anger?

_____

_____

_____

_____

_____

_____

_____

_____

_____

_____

_____

"How can you waste time? You have only so much to use,
and no matter what you do, it still passes."
Felix Salten

Day 83 - What places always make you feel at home?

_____

_____

_____

_____

_____

_____

_____

_____

_____

_____

_____

Day 84 - What would happen this month if you would commit to being honest with yourself and other people?

_____

_____

_____

_____

_____

_____

_____

_____

_____

_____

_____

"Perhaps it is better to wake up after all, even to suffer,
rather than to remain a dupe to illusions all one's life."
Kate Chopin

Day 85 -Which desires are hidden beneath your surface?

_____
_____
_____
_____
_____
_____
_____
_____
_____
_____
_____
_____
_____

Day 86 -Which deep desire makes you feel ashamed of yourself?

_____
_____
_____
_____
_____
_____
_____
_____
_____
_____
_____
_____

"To swallow and follow, whether old doctrine or new propaganda,
is a weakness still dominating the human mind."
Charlotte Perkins Gilman

Day 87 -What does your shadow look like?

_____
_____
_____
_____
_____
_____
_____
_____
_____
_____
_____

Day 88 -What would happen if you would make peace with your
shadow side and embrace it as part of who you are?

_____
_____
_____
_____
_____
_____
_____
_____
_____
_____
_____
_____

"Tell me and I forget, teach me and I may remember,
involve me and I learn."
Benjamin Franklin

Day 89 - What lessons did you learn the past three months?

_____

_____

_____

_____

_____

_____

_____

_____

Day 90 - *Comfort zone +++++.*
"Are you really happy, or just comfortable?"
What is one big thing you could do this month to expand your comfort
zone? Think about what you've always wanted to do. Write down when
and how you are going to do *this month* and put it on your calendar.
(Examples are, joining an acting class, buying tickets for a city trip,
writing the first chapter of a novel or non-fiction book, organizing a
party for friends, attending a speed dating event)

_____

_____

_____

_____

_____

_____

_____

_____

"A gift consists not in what is done or given,
but in the intention of the giver or doer."
Seneca

Day 91 - What would the most courageous, kind and strongest version of
yourself do this month?

_____

_____

_____

_____

_____

_____

_____

_____

_____

_____

Day 92 - What would the most courageous, kind and strongest version
of yourself do this week?

_____

_____

_____

_____

_____

_____

_____

_____

_____

_____

> "Our life is frittered away by detail. Simplify, simplify."
> Henry David Thoreau

Day 93 - What would the most courageous, kind and strongest version of yourself do today?

_____

_____

_____

_____

_____

_____

_____

_____

_____

_____

Day 94 - What one creative talent would you like to develop? Come up with at least three different things you could do to make this happen.

_____

_____

_____

_____

_____

_____

_____

_____

_____

_____

"We are like islands in the sea,
separate on the surface but connected in the deep."
William James

Day 95 - Pick one of your answers from yesterday and make it happen. Write down how you're going to develop your creative talent for at least one week and how you're going to hold yourself accountable.

_____

_____

_____

_____

_____

_____

_____

_____

_____

_____

Day 96 - What would change if you knew that _The Universe_ was on your side?

_____

_____

_____

_____

_____

_____

_____

_____

_____

_____

"It is unwise to be too sure of one's own wisdom.
It is healthy to be reminded that the strongest might weaken
and the wisest might err."
Mahatma Gandhi

Day 97 - What happens if you deny the demands of your inner being?

Day 98 - Is your sexual energy enriching your life
or is it enslaving you?

"Bring me the sunset in a cup."
Emily Dickinson

Day 99 - What are three things you could do to build a healthier and more passionate sex life?

_____

_____

_____

_____

_____

_____

_____

_____

_____

_____

_____

Day 100 -What is one thing you could do this week to make you feel more attractive?

_____

_____

_____

_____

_____

_____

_____

_____

_____

_____

_____

> "I'm the one that's got to die when it's time for me to die, so let me live my life the way I want to."
> Jimi Hendrix

Day 101 -What is your true calling?

_____
_____
_____
_____
_____
_____
_____
_____
_____
_____
_____

Day 102 - What book have you always wanted to read?
How could you read it within 3 months?

_____
_____
_____
_____
_____
_____
_____
_____
_____
_____

"A friend to all is a friend to none."
Aristotle

Day 103 - What part of yourself do you hate? Why?

Day 104 - How could you be more kind
to the part of yourself you hate?

"I've got the key to my castle in the air,
but whether I can unlock the door remains to be seen."
Louisa May Alcott

Day 105 -If you were ten percent more productive,
how would last week be different?

_____
_____
_____
_____
_____
_____
_____
_____
_____
_____

Day 106 -If you were ten percent more productive,
how could this week be different?

_____
_____
_____
_____
_____
_____
_____
_____
_____
_____

"Losing your way on a journey is unfortunate.
But, losing your reason for the journey is a fate more cruel."
H.G.Wells

Day 107 -In what area in your life do you find it difficult to find balance?

_____
_____
_____
_____
_____
_____
_____
_____
_____
_____
_____

Day 108 - What does being busy and a lack of faith have to do with each other?

_____
_____
_____
_____
_____
_____
_____
_____
_____
_____
_____
_____

"Wisdom is the fruit of a balanced development."
Alfred North Whitehead

Day 109 - What is one thing you could do today to treat yourself?
Go ahead and do it.

_____

_____

_____

_____

_____

_____

_____

_____

_____

_____

_____

Day 110 -How do you feel when people compliment you?

_____

_____

_____

_____

_____

_____

_____

_____

_____

_____

_____

"The bird that would soar above the level plain of tradition
and prejudice must have strong wings."
Kate Chopin

Day 111 -Why would people underestimate you?

Day 112 -Why would people overestimate you?

"Hungry man, reach for the book: it is a weapon."
Bertolt Brecht

Day 113 - What makes you shy?

_____

_____

_____

_____

_____

_____

_____

_____

_____

_____

Day 114 - What about your body makes you feel grateful?
Try to come up with at least five things.

_____

_____

_____

_____

_____

_____

_____

_____

_____

_____

_____

> "I call people rich
> when they're able to meet the requirements of their imagination."
> Henry James

Day 115 - What about your current life situation makes you feel grateful? Try to come up with at least five things.

Day 116 - What fears have a devastating effect on your life?

"If you look the right way,
you can see that the whole world is a garden."
Frances Hodgson Burnett

Day 117 - Take a look at your life of yesterday. Pick the fear that has the most devastating effect. Come up with at least three better ways to deal with this fear.

_____

_____

_____

_____

_____

_____

_____

_____

_____

_____

_____

Day 118 - What is distracting you?

_____

_____

_____

_____

_____

_____

_____

_____

_____

_____

_____

> "I always arrive late at the office,
> but I make up for it by leaving early."
> Charles Lamb

Day 119 - What are three ways to work smarter instead of harder?

_____
_____
_____
_____
_____
_____
_____
_____
_____
_____
_____

Day 120 - In hindsight, what would you have done differently
last month?

_____
_____
_____
_____
_____
_____
_____
_____
_____
_____

"We need never be ashamed of our tears."
Charles Dickens

Day 121 - *Monthly challenge.*
What are three ways to make this month more successful than last month? Write down what, when and how you are going to do it and put it on your calendar.

_____

_____

_____

_____

_____

_____

_____

_____

_____

_____

_____

Day 122 - Where do your beliefs about learning take you five years from now?

_____

_____

_____

_____

_____

_____

_____

_____

_____

_____

_____

"There is no exquisite beauty...
without some strangeness in the proportion."
Edgar Allan Poe

Day 123 - What is the one thing you could do today that will make you feel satisfied?

_____

_____

_____

_____

_____

_____

_____

_____

_____

_____

Day 124 - What makes you worry about your financial situation?

_____

_____

_____

_____

_____

_____

_____

_____

_____

_____

"Laughter is sunshine,
it chases winter from the human face."
Victor Hugo

Day 125 - What is one tiny thing that you could do
to improve your financial situation?

_____
_____
_____
_____
_____
_____
_____
_____
_____
_____

Day 126 - How is the way you are trying to _protect_ yourself
hurting your love life?

_____
_____
_____
_____
_____
_____
_____
_____
_____
_____
_____

"Nature is pleased with simplicity.
And nature is no dummy."
Isaac Newton

Day 127 - How could being *more open* improve your love life?

Day 128 - Why do you want to improve yourself?

"I have absolutely no pleasure in the stimulants in which I sometimes so madly indulge. It has not been in the pursuit of pleasure that I have periled life and reputation and reason. It has been the desperate attempt to escape from torturing memories, from a sense of insupportable loneliness and a dread of some strange impending doom."
J.K. Rowling

Day 129 - What past failure actually proved to be a blessing?

_____

_____

_____

_____

_____

_____

_____

_____

_____

_____

Day 130 - Describe what living _the ideal life_ means to you.

_____

_____

_____

_____

_____

_____

_____

_____

_____

_____

_____

"Is it really possible to tell someone else
what one feels?"

Leo Tolstoy

Day 131 - What is standing between your life right now
and your ideal life?

_____

_____

_____

_____

_____

_____

_____

_____

_____

_____

Day 132 - Are your expectations too high or are you afraid to get out of
your comfort zone?

_____

_____

_____

_____

_____

_____

_____

_____

_____

_____

"I am the master of my fate:
I am the captain of my soul."
William Ernest Henley

Day 133 - What worries occupy your mind?

_____

_____

_____

_____

_____

_____

_____

_____

_____

_____

Day 134 - What one small habit could change your life for the habit?
Pick one and describe how you are going to integrate it in your life. Try
it for at least five days. (Examples: making your bed, drinking water
instead of soft drinks, meditating for five minutes a day)

_____

_____

_____

_____

_____

_____

_____

_____

_____

_____

_____

"The art of being wise is knowing what to overlook."

William James

Day 135 - Are your desires coming from your ego or your heart?

Day 136 - When do you feel you are wasting time?

"The morning was full of sunlight and hope."
Kate Chopin

Day 137 - Write down at least one different approach to turn your sadness into a feeling of hope.

_____

_____

_____

_____

_____

_____

_____

_____

_____

_____

Day 138 - Name at least three experiences that made you feel great about yourself.

_____

_____

_____

_____

_____

_____

_____

_____

_____

_____

_____

"Not all of us can do great things.
But we can do small things with great love."
Mother Teresa

Day 139 - What is one lesson you learned about yourself
in the past year?

_____
_____
_____
_____
_____
_____
_____
_____
_____
_____

Day 140 - What three things made you feel grateful yesterday?

_____
_____
_____
_____
_____
_____
_____
_____
_____
_____
_____
_____

"Life is like riding a bicycle.
To keep your balance, you must keep moving."
Albert Einstein

Day 141 - Where do thoughts actually come from?

_____

_____

_____

_____

_____

_____

_____

_____

_____

Day 142 - Write down three ways you could treat yourself more often, without feeling guilty.

_____

_____

_____

_____

_____

_____

_____

_____

_____

_____

_____

"If I had a flower for every time I thought of you...
I could walk through my garden forever."
Alfred Tennyson

Day 143 - Which doubts require your attention?

Day 144 - Is time going too fast?

"Happiness is like a butterfly which, when pursued, is always beyond our grasp, but, if you will sit down quietly, may alight upon you."
Nathaniel Hawthorne

Day 145 - When did you feel most happy?

Day 146 -What do you do to *escape* uncomfortable feelings?

"For after the Battle comes quiet."
H.G. Wells

Day 147 - Meditation is proven to have amazing benefits, such as calming your mind, increasing productivity and feelings of happiness and gratitude.Try to meditate this week for five minutes a day. Write down below how and when you are going to practice meditation this week. (tip for this week, a 5-minute guided meditation https://www.youtube.com/watch?v=i50ZAs7v9es)

Day 148 - What makes you feel uncertain about yourself?

"By numbing the pain it only comes back bigger.
C.W. V. Straaten

Day 149 - What would other people find attractive about you?

_____

_____

_____

_____

_____

_____

_____

_____

_____

_____

_____

Day 150 - What could you do to prepare yourself for success / better times?

_____

_____

_____

_____

_____

_____

_____

_____

_____

_____

_____

"The best things in life make you sweaty."
Edgar Allan Poe

Day 151 - Who has always been there for you?

Day 152 -How did Hollywood movies influence your view on romance?

"I am no bird; and no net ensnares me:
I am a free human being with an independent will."
Charlotte Brontë, *Jane Eyre*

Day 153 - What clouds your judgment?

_____
_____
_____
_____
_____
_____
_____
_____
_____

Day 154 - If you could rewrite the next chapter of your life right now, what would it look like?

_____
_____
_____
_____
_____
_____
_____
_____
_____
_____
_____

"It is well to be up before daybreak,
for such habits contribute to health, wealth, and wisdom."
Aristotle

Day 155 -Comfort zone +++++

The comfort zone challenge this week is to wake up one hour earlier than normal and do something that will empower your day. Write down what you're going to do and when. (Examples: meditation, walking, running, finishing or starting your most important task of the day, a fine morning routine)

Day 156 - How could you deal with your worries in a more constructive manner?

"The best way to avert misfortune is to deal with it before it's born."
Sun Tzu, *The Art of War*

Day 157 - What problems are lying ahead?

_____

_____

_____

_____

_____

_____

_____

_____

Day 158 - In a Life Box you compile all the different areas of your life. This gives you a clear overview of your life. For example:

Family	Love Life
Friends & Social Life	Finances
Career	Sports & Health
Personal Development	Spirituality
Traveling	Contribution

Today's exercise is to make a Life Box for yourself, on the next blank page. Mostly it will consist of 8 to 12 different areas. Have some fun with it and create a good overview of your life.

(Our Life Box is just an example; you could have a totally different one. Also we have combined *Sports & Health* together. If sporting is a big part of your life, it would make more sense to separate *Sports & Health* into a different box.)

"It is better to fail in originality than to succeed in imitation."
Herman Melville

Day 159 - *Life Box.*
The next exercise is to rank each box. Number 1 being the most important and so on. Rank what you value the most, not where you spend the most time on. There are two blank pages added to do the Day 159 and 160 exercises properly.

Day 160 - *Life Box.*
Now rank the box again, but different.
Where you spend the most time is number one, and so on.

"You'll never find a rainbow if you're looking down."
Charlie Chaplin

Day 161 - *Life Box.*
Look at your answers from yesterday and the day before. What do you value and where do you spend the most time on corresponding? Which area(s) are most out of balance?

_____

_____

_____

_____

_____

_____

_____

_____

_____

_____

Day 162 - How does it honestly, really feel when people close to you have success?

_____

_____

_____

_____

_____

_____

_____

_____

_____

_____

"But feelings can't be ignored,
no matter how unjust or ungrateful they seem."
Anne Frank, *The Diary of a Young Girl*

Day 163 - What skills have you developed over the years?

_____
_____
_____
_____
_____
_____
_____
_____
_____
_____
_____

Day 164 - What feelings do you resist?

_____
_____
_____
_____
_____
_____
_____
_____
_____
_____
_____
_____

"Do what you feel in your heart to be right –
for you'll be criticized anyway."
Eleanor Roosevelt

Day 165 - What thought patterns are harming you?

_____
_____
_____
_____
_____
_____
_____
_____
_____
_____
_____

Day 166 - Do you feel sorry for people who are in a worse situation
than yourself?

_____
_____
_____
_____
_____
_____
_____
_____
_____
_____
_____
_____

"Every man has his secret sorrows which the world knows not; and often times we call a man cold when he is only sad."
Henry Wadsworth Longfellow

Day 167 - When do you feel sorry for yourself?

_____

Day 168 - What kind of imaginations help you through the day?

_____

"I am a part of all that I have met."
Alfred Tennyson

Day 169 - Write down at least five things you're grateful for.

_____

_____

_____

_____

_____

_____

_____

_____

_____

_____

_____

Day 170 - Do you often make impulsive purchases?

_____

_____

_____

_____

_____

_____

_____

_____

_____

_____

_____

_____

"It is not down on any map; true places never are."
Herman Melville

Day 171 - Do you feel like you can't burden other people with your problems?

_____
_____
_____
_____
_____
_____
_____
_____
_____
_____
_____

Day 172 - What is your opinion on charitable donations?

_____
_____
_____
_____
_____
_____
_____
_____
_____
_____
_____

"We first make our habits, then our habits make us."
John Dryden

Day 173 - If you would meet your 21-year old self in a bar tonight, what is the one piece of advice you would give?

_____

_____

_____

_____

_____

_____

_____

_____

_____

_____

Day 174 - Do you honestly and really listen to people when they're telling you about their problems? If not, where do you think about?

_____

_____

_____

_____

_____

_____

_____

_____

_____

_____

_____

"There is nothing in the world so irresistibly contagious as laughter and good humor."
Charles Dickens

Day 175 - What makes you laugh?
Try to come up with at least five things.

Day 176 - Do you constantly want to grow as a person?
Why or why not?

"Be kind, for everyone you meet is fighting a harder battle."
Plato

Day 177 - Is 24 hours in the day enough for you? Why or why not?

_____

_____

_____

_____

_____

_____

_____

_____

_____

_____

_____

Day 178 - What makes you suspicious of other people?

_____

_____

_____

_____

_____

_____

_____

_____

_____

_____

_____

_____

"All that we see or seem is but a dream within a dream."

Edgar Allan Poe

Day 179 - Imagine you time traveled back to the past… You gazed upon your 5-year old self. How does he or she feel and look?

Day 180 - Do you have a recurring dream? If so, what could it mean?

"The universe is change; our life is what our thoughts make it."
Marcus Aurelius

Day 181 - *Monthly challenge.*
Write down at least five things you could do, without feeling guilty, to
make this month more enjoyable than last month. Examples are
treating yourself to a Netflix night, going on a date, cooking dinner for
friends, a walk in nature, taking more rest, buying new clothes,
watching more comedy, etc. Write down how you are going to follow
through with doing these things.

_____

_____

_____

_____

_____

_____

_____

_____

_____

_____

Day 182 - What political issue stirs you up with emotion?

_____

_____

_____

_____

_____

_____

_____

_____

_____

"Rather than love, than money, than fame, give me truth."
Henry David Thoreau

Day 183 - How could you spend more money on experiences than on things?

_____
_____
_____
_____
_____
_____
_____
_____
_____
_____

Day 184 - Is it true that you mustn't take life too seriously? Why or why not?

_____
_____
_____
_____
_____
_____
_____
_____
_____
_____
_____

"And those who were seen dancing were thought to be insane by those who could not hear the music."
Friedrich Nietzsche

Day 185 - How do you adapt to new situations?

Day 186 - If you had only two days to live,
what would you regret not seeing?

"A faithful friend is a strong defense;
And he that hath found him hath found a treasure."
Louisa May Alcott

Day 187 - What makes a good friend?

Day 188 - Is it time for a career change?

"Everyone sees what you appear to be,
few experience what you really are."
Niccolò Machiavelli

Day 189 - Do you sometimes feel superior to other people?
When and why?

_____

_____

_____

_____

_____

_____

_____

_____

_____

_____

Day 190 - What is one thing you could do this week to improve your
energy level?

_____

_____

_____

_____

_____

_____

_____

_____

_____

_____

_____

"It is love alone that gives worth to all things."
St. Teresa of Avila

Day 191 - Do you find it important to win a discussion, or does it matter more that no one gets upset?

Day 192 - What three things made you feel grateful yesterday?

> "Let us read, and let us dance;
> these two amusements will never do any harm to the world."
> Voltaire

Day 193 - Do you feel you often have to justify yourself to other people? If so, how come?

_____
_____
_____
_____
_____
_____
_____
_____
_____
_____
_____
_____

Day 194 - If you could change one rule of social conditioning, what would it be and why?

_____
_____
_____
_____
_____
_____
_____
_____
_____
_____
_____
_____

"Love turns work into rest."
Teresa of Avila

Day 195 - What accomplishment of last week made you proud?

_____

_____

_____

_____

_____

_____

_____

_____

_____

_____

Day 196 - Do you like to be the center of attention? Why or why not?

_____

_____

_____

_____

_____

_____

_____

_____

_____

_____

_____

_____

"Success is not final, failure is not fatal:
it is the courage to continue that counts."
Winston S. Churchill

Day 197 - What is one thing you could do this week to improve your financial situation?

_____

_____

_____

_____

_____

_____

_____

_____

_____

_____

Day 198 - Are you the average of your five closest friends?

_____

_____

_____

_____

_____

_____

_____

_____

_____

_____

_____

"Re-examine all you have been told.
Dismiss what insults your soul."
Walt Whitman

Day 199 - If you could unlearn one thought pattern or behavior, what would it be?

_____

_____

_____

_____

_____

_____

_____

_____

_____

_____

_____

Day 200 - What role does _ego_ play in your life?

_____

_____

_____

_____

_____

_____

_____

_____

_____

_____

_____

"There are more people who wish to be loved
than there are who are willing to love."
Nicolas Chamfort

Day 201 - How could you help to improve humanity?

_____
_____
_____
_____
_____
_____
_____
_____
_____
_____
_____

Day 202 - When was the last time you felt truly alive?

_____
_____
_____
_____
_____
_____
_____
_____
_____
_____
_____

"Your task is not to seek for love, but merely to seek and find all the barriers within yourself that you have built against it."
Rumi

Day 203 - What do you have to offer your (potential) partner in a relationship?

_____

_____

_____

_____

_____

_____

_____

_____

_____

_____

Day 204 - *Comfort zone ++++++*
Go this week for at least 24 hours without using your phone.
Write down below what is holding you back the most and how you could minimize the *damage* when not using your phone for 24 hours.

_____

_____

_____

_____

_____

_____

_____

_____

_____

_____

"Every saint has a past, and every sinner has a future."
Oscar Wilde

Day 205 - How do you deal with rejection?

_____
_____
_____
_____
_____
_____
_____
_____
_____
_____

Day 206 - What would a perfect date look like?

_____
_____
_____
_____
_____
_____
_____
_____
_____
_____
_____
_____

"Vision is the art of seeing things invisible."
Jonathan Swift

Day 207 - Do you find it difficult to start a conversation?
Why or why not?

_____

_____

_____

_____

_____

_____

_____

_____

_____

Day 208 - What about your job gives you energy?
And what about your job costs you energy?

_____

_____

_____

_____

_____

_____

_____

_____

_____

_____

_____

"Stop thinking, and end your problems."
Lao Tzu

Day 209 - If someone else knew all the things you've experienced in the past, what advice would she give you?

_____

_____

_____

_____

_____

_____

_____

_____

_____

_____

Day 210 - What is all that you've accomplished this month? What lesson did you learn this month? What is one thing that you could've done better this month?

_____

_____

_____

_____

_____

_____

_____

_____

_____

_____

_____

"I have no special talents. I am only passionately curious."
Albert Einstein

Day 211 - What is the one thing you could do that would make this month great? How are you going to make certain that you will follow through?

Day 212 - What thoughts are you suppressing?

"There is a pleasure in the pathless woods"
Lord Byron

Day 213 - What would you miss if you stopped using your smartphone for 48 hours?

_____
_____
_____
_____
_____
_____
_____
_____
_____
_____

Day 214 - What parts of your life actually don't reflect who you are?

_____
_____
_____
_____
_____
_____
_____
_____
_____
_____
_____
_____

"I have decided to stick to love...Hate is too great a burden to bear."
Martin Luther King Jr.

Day 215 - What is the one thing you could do today,
to live a better tomorrow?

Day 216 - What kind of life do you think you deserve?
Is it far away from the life you are living now?

"A thing is not necessarily true because a man dies for it."
Oscar Wilde

Day 217 - What kind of people irritate you?
(Name at least three characteristics or behaviors)

_____
_____
_____
_____
_____
_____
_____
_____
_____
_____

Day 218 - What kind of people do you look up to?
(Name at least three characteristics or behaviors)

_____
_____
_____
_____
_____
_____
_____
_____
_____
_____
_____

"You have power over your mind - not outside events.
Realize this, and you will find strength."
Marcus Aurelius

Day 219 - What are the characteristics of your perfect partner?

_____
_____
_____
_____
_____
_____
_____
_____
_____
_____
_____

Day 220 - If you could change one thing about your past,
what would it be?

_____
_____
_____
_____
_____
_____
_____
_____
_____
_____
_____

> "I dream my painting and I paint my dream."
> Vincent van Gogh

Day 221 - How could you be seduced?

_____

_____

_____

_____

_____

_____

_____

_____

_____

_____

_____

Day 222 - What one sentence would describe you best?

_____

_____

_____

_____

_____

_____

_____

_____

_____

_____

_____

_____

"I go to seek a Great Perhaps."
François Rabelais

Day 223 - With what behavior you don't trust yourself? Why?

_____

_____

_____

_____

_____

_____

_____

_____

_____

_____

Day 224 - How is the way you treat your body going to affect you 10 years from now? And in 20 years?

_____

_____

_____

_____

_____

_____

_____

_____

_____

_____

_____

_____

"It is health that is real wealth and not pieces of gold and silver."
Mahatma Gandhi

Day 225 - What is the one thing you could do this week to take care of your body? How are you going to make sure to follow through? (It could also be something small: 15 minutes of exercise, water instead of soda drinks, fast food only once a week)

_____

_____

_____

_____

_____

_____

_____

_____

_____

_____

Day 226 - Are you doing things out of loyalty that actually don't feel good?

_____

_____

_____

_____

_____

_____

_____

_____

_____

_____

"Let nothing perturb you, nothing frighten you.
All things pass.
God does not change.
Patience achieves everything."
Saint Teresa of Avila

Day 227 - What is the difference between love and loyalty?

_____

_____

_____

_____

_____

_____

_____

_____

_____

_____

Day 228 - What rules of society block you from living the life that you want?

_____

_____

_____

_____

_____

_____

_____

_____

_____

_____

_____

"Heard melodies are sweet,
but those unheard, are sweeter"
John Keats

Day 229 - What people in your life cause a good deal of your
overall happiness?

_____

_____

_____

_____

_____

_____

_____

_____

_____

_____

Day 230 - When was the last time you read a book that influenced you
in a serious way?

_____

_____

_____

_____

_____

_____

_____

_____

_____

_____

"It's no use going back to yesterday,
because I was a different person then."
Lewis Carroll

Day 231 - Write down at least ten little things that make you happy.

_____
_____
_____
_____
_____
_____
_____
_____
_____
_____
_____

Day 232 - What would happen if for the next three days you did the
opposite of the majority of people?

_____
_____
_____
_____
_____
_____
_____
_____
_____
_____
_____
_____

"Whether you think you can, or you think you can't--you're right."
Henry Ford

Day 233 - How could you be a better friend to yourself?

_____

_____

_____

_____

_____

_____

_____

_____

_____

_____

_____

Day 234 -What five things are you grateful for in your life right now?

_____

_____

_____

_____

_____

_____

_____

_____

_____

_____

_____

"Think of all the beauty still left around you and be happy."
Anne Frank

Day 234 - What parts of your body feel tight?

Day 236 - *Catching your critical thoughts.*
Write down the most common self-critical thoughts you have.

"The trouble is, you think you have time."
Buddha

Day 237 - Look at your list of yesterday.
How would your life change if you were ten percent more kind to yourself? And how would your life change if, instead of criticizing, you accepted your flaws and worked on your strengths?

_____

_____

_____

_____

_____

_____

_____

_____

_____

_____

_____

Day 238 - Could you be alone without feeling lonely?

_____

_____

_____

_____

_____

_____

_____

_____

_____

"The mind is everything. What you think you become."
Buddha

Day 239 - *Enjoy moments.*
What are 10 little things you enjoy? Make sure that every day this week
you do one of these things. To make yourself accountable, put on your
calendar *"enjoy moments"* every day.

_____

Day 240 - How is complaining making your life more negative? Make
the commitment to at least stop complaining for the next 24 hours.

_____

"Believe nothing you hear, and only one half that you see."
Edgar Allan Poe

Day 241 - *Comfort zone +++++++*
Have a notebook and a pen next to you so you can write your dream down right away. Be conscious about your dreaming. For the rest of this week when you wake up write down your dream of that night. If you have trouble remembering your dreams; when you wake up try to hold your eyes closed for a moment. And ask yourself, *What just happened?*

_____

_____

_____

_____

_____

_____

_____

_____

_____

_____

Day 242 - Describe what physical sensations and thoughts you have when you feel lonely?

_____

_____

_____

_____

_____

_____

_____

_____

_____

"There is nothing either good or bad, but thinking makes it so."
William Shakespeare, *Hamlet*

Day 243 - What politically incorrect thoughts are you scared to express?

_____
_____
_____
_____
_____
_____
_____
_____
_____
_____
_____

Day 244 - What do you look forward to in the near future?

_____
_____
_____
_____
_____
_____
_____
_____
_____
_____
_____

"By failing to prepare, you are preparing to fail."
Benjamin Franklin

Day 245 - What inspires you?

_____
_____
_____
_____
_____
_____
_____
_____
_____
_____
_____

Day 246 - Plan out tomorrow exactly as you would want it to be, and then try to follow it as closely as you can.

_____
_____
_____
_____
_____
_____
_____
_____
_____
_____

"That it will never come again is what makes life so sweet."
Emily Dickinson

Day 247 - *Recap.*
How did the planning and following through go?
What are your three most important insights?

_____
_____
_____
_____
_____
_____
_____
_____
_____
_____

Day 248 - What does being rich mean to you?

_____
_____
_____
_____
_____
_____
_____
_____
_____
_____
_____

"Education is the most powerful weapon
which you can use to change the world."
Nelson Mandela

Day 249 - What does being poor mean to you? How can you avoid
becoming poor / working your way out of being poor?

_____

_____

_____

_____

_____

_____

_____

_____

_____

_____

Day 250 - What are three things other people can learn from you
in terms of finances?

_____

_____

_____

_____

_____

_____

_____

_____

_____

_____

"Painting is poetry that is seen rather than felt,
and poetry is painting that is felt rather than seen."
Leonardo da Vinci

Day 251 - What age would you like to be now? Why?

Day 252 - Do you often have the feeling that your life is run by others?
Why or why not?

"Do not be afraid;
our fate Cannot be taken from us; it is a gift."
Dante Alighieri

Day 253 - If you were the most courageous, kind and strongest version of yourself, what is the one thing you would do today?

_____

_____

_____

_____

_____

_____

_____

_____

_____

_____

Day 254 -What makes you feel weak about yourself?
What is one thing you could do to change this right now?

_____

_____

_____

_____

_____

_____

_____

_____

_____

_____

"The future belongs to those who believe in the beauty of their dreams."
Eleanor Roosevelt

Day 255 - What action(s) are you postponing?

Day 256 - Do you find life demanding? Why or why not?

"Courage is the first of human qualities
because it is the quality which guarantees the others."
Aristotle

Day 257 - What would you like to do more often?

_____
_____
_____
_____
_____
_____
_____
_____
_____
_____

Day 258 - How would your life change if you kept reminding yourself
that everyone is doing the best they can?

_____
_____
_____
_____
_____
_____
_____
_____
_____

"Those who have not found the heaven below, will fail of it above."
Emily Dickinson

Day 259 - What one creative talent would you like to develop?
Come up with at least three different things you could do
to make this happen.

Day 260 -Pick one of your answers from yesterday and make it happen.
Write down how you're going to develop your creative talent for at least
one week and how you're going to hold yourself accountable.

"Not being heard is no reason for silence."
Victor Hugo

Day 261 - What role does work play in the life you desire?

_____

_____

_____

_____

_____

_____

_____

_____

_____

_____

Day 262 - What does being a man / woman / transgender mean to you?

_____

_____

_____

_____

_____

_____

_____

_____

_____

_____

_____

"You can turn over a new leaf every hour if you choose."
Arnold Bennett

Day 263 - Which mistakes do you constantly repeat when it comes to being your own best friend?

_____

_____

_____

_____

_____

_____

_____

_____

_____

_____

_____

Day 264 - How would the people closest to you describe you?

_____

_____

_____

_____

_____

_____

_____

_____

_____

_____

_____

_____

"All the darkness in the world
cannot extinguish the light of a single candle."
St. Francis Of Assisi

Day 265 - How would you like the people closest to you to
describe you?

_____

_____

_____

_____

_____

_____

_____

_____

_____

_____

_____

Day 266 - What role does pleasing others play in your life?

_____

_____

_____

_____

_____

_____

_____

_____

_____

_____

_____

"Quiet minds cannot be perplexed or frightened
but go on in fortune or misfortune at their own private pace,
like a clock during a thunderstorm."
Robert Louis Stevenson

Day 267 - What would happen if you stop pleasing others for the next 48 hours?

_____

_____

_____

_____

_____

_____

_____

_____

_____

Day 268 - What are three more constructive things you could do than pleasing others?

_____

_____

_____

_____

_____

_____

_____

_____

_____

_____

_____

"I prefer to be true to myself, even at the hazard of incurring the ridicule of others, rather than to be false, and to incur my own abhorrence."
Frederick Douglass

Day 269 - What are three things other people can learn from you when it comes to personal relationships?

Day 270 - What reasons, hidden in your subconscious, actually prevent you from living a successful and happy life?

"Beauty is not caused. It is."
Emily Dickinson

Day 271 - If you had $200 million dollars in the bank, what would the rest of this month look like?

_____

_____

_____

_____

_____

_____

_____

_____

_____

Day 272 - *Monthly challenge.*
What area of your life do you want to improve this month?
What is one tiny thing that you could do this month to improve this specific area? (examples: *health*, eating an apple a day / don't drink soft drinks on weekdays, *finances,* track everything you spend on an Excel sheet and reflect on it at the end of the month / reading one financial self development book this month.)
Commit with yourself to do this on a daily basis for this month.
Write down how you are going to hold yourself accountable.

_____

_____

_____

_____

_____

_____

_____

_____

_____

"Everything's a story - You are a story -I am a story."
Frances Hodgson Burnett

Day 273 - What were you grateful for last week?

_____

_____

_____

_____

_____

_____

_____

_____

_____

Day 274 - What are two things you could do this week to improve
your self-confidence?

_____

_____

_____

_____

_____

_____

_____

_____

_____

_____

"The only real parting is when there is no love left to part from"
Dinah Craik

Day 275 - If you could reverse one experience or one habit in your life, which would it be?

_____
_____
_____
_____
_____
_____
_____
_____
_____
_____
_____

Day 276 - What is giving you a feeling of restlessness?

_____
_____
_____
_____
_____
_____
_____
_____
_____
_____
_____
_____

> "The rights of every man are diminished
> when the rights of one man are threatened."
> John F. Kennedy

Day 277 - What leads your life, your intuition or your mind? Why?

_____
_____
_____
_____
_____
_____
_____
_____
_____
_____

Day 278 - What three things you could do to build a deeper connection with the people closest to you?

_____
_____
_____
_____
_____
_____
_____
_____
_____
_____
_____
_____

"A loving heart is the beginning of all knowledge."
Thomas Carlyle

Day 279 - What is one thing other people can learn from you when it comes to self-development?

_____

_____

_____

_____

_____

_____

_____

_____

_____

_____

Day 280 - In what area of your life could you use some external help?

_____

_____

_____

_____

_____

_____

_____

_____

_____

_____

_____

_____

"Never close your lips
to those whom you have already opened your heart."
Charles Dickens

Day 281 - What are two things you could do this week to improve
your conversations?

_____
_____
_____
_____
_____
_____
_____
_____
_____

Day 282 - How could you spend more quality time
with the people closest to you?

_____
_____
_____
_____
_____
_____
_____
_____
_____
_____

"And remember, no matter where you go, there you are."
Confucius

Day 283 - What makes life a blessing?

Day 284 - What makes life hard for you?

""The way is not in the sky.
The way is in the heart."
Buddha

Day 285 - What do all teenagers have to learn about life?

_____

_____

_____

_____

_____

_____

_____

_____

_____

_____

Day 286 - Are your goals motivating you or are they giving you stress?

_____

_____

_____

_____

_____

_____

_____

_____

_____

_____

"Live in the sunshine, swim the sea, drink the wild air."
Ralph Waldo Emerson

Day 287 - What is the one thing you would like to learn before you die?

_____
_____
_____
_____
_____
_____
_____
_____
_____
_____

Day 288 - *Comfort zone ++++++++*
Take a cold shower this week for at least 30 seconds this week. Reflect on it, on this page. For now, write down when you are going to do it and put it down in your calendar.

_____
_____
_____
_____
_____
_____
_____
_____
_____
_____
_____
_____

"Opinion is a fitting thing but truth outlasts the sun -
if then we cannot own them both, possess the oldest one."
Emily Dickinson

Day 289 - What about your life
would make other people jealous?

_____
_____
_____
_____
_____
_____
_____
_____
_____
_____

Day 290 - In what area in your life
do you actually need to be more selfish?

_____
_____
_____
_____
_____
_____
_____
_____
_____

"Dwell on the beauty of life.
Watch the stars, and see yourself running with them."
Marcus Aurelius

Day 291 -What does being in a loving relationship mean to you?

_____
_____
_____
_____
_____
_____
_____
_____
_____
_____
_____

Day 292 - In what other country would you like to live and why?

_____
_____
_____
_____
_____
_____
_____
_____
_____
_____
_____
_____

"Be ye strong therefore, and let not your hands be weak:
for your work shall be rewarded."
2 Chronicles 15:7 (KJV)

Day 293 - What kind of mentor do you need in your life right now?

_____

_____

_____

_____

_____

_____

_____

_____

_____

_____

_____

Day 294 - What does your body need right now?

_____

_____

_____

_____

_____

_____

_____

_____

_____

_____

_____

"Never give up... No one knows what's going to happen next."
L. Frank Baum

Day 295 - If you knew nobody would judge you,
how would this week be different?

_____
_____
_____
_____
_____
_____
_____
_____
_____
_____
_____

Day 296 - What in your life right now would you like to show your old
high school class?

_____
_____
_____
_____
_____
_____
_____
_____
_____
_____
_____
_____

"Do you not see how necessary a world of pains
and troubles is to school an intelligence and make it a soul?"
John Keats

Day 297 - What is one past failure that is still hurting you?
How could you deal better with this past failure in the next seven days?
Write down at least two solutions.

_____

_____

_____

_____

_____

_____

_____

_____

_____

_____

Day 298 - What would you do tomorrow
if there were only 12 hours in the day?

_____

_____

_____

_____

_____

_____

_____

_____

_____

"I have always thought the actions of men
the best interpreters of their thoughts."
John Locke

Day 299 - What makes you jealous of other people?

_____
_____
_____
_____
_____
_____
_____
_____
_____
_____
_____

Day 300 - In what area in your life do you most compare yourself with
other people? Why?

_____
_____
_____
_____
_____
_____
_____
_____
_____
_____
_____

"If you are irritated by every rub, how will your mirror be polished?"
Rumi

Day 301 - *Monthly challenge*
The famous *Pareto principle*, named after an Italian economist, states that 80% of the effects roughly are the result of 20% of the causes. It is the law of the vital few. What 20% of work brought you 80% of last month's results? What is one thing you could do to make this month more productive than the previous one? Write it down and also come up with how you are going to follow through.

_____

_____

_____

_____

_____

_____

_____

_____

_____

_____

Day 302 - Are you a good example for the people closest to you?

_____

_____

_____

_____

_____

_____

_____

_____

_____

"Stop choosing the wrong path, when you know better."
Zen Mirrors

Day 303 - In what area(s) of your life are you more or less following the crowd, instead of listening to your own intuition?

_____
_____
_____
_____
_____
_____
_____
_____
_____
_____

Day 304 - What has made this year so far different than all the years before?

_____
_____
_____
_____
_____
_____
_____
_____
_____
_____
_____

"The course of true love never did run smooth."
William Shakespeare

Day 305 - Which people don't treat you with the love and respect
you really deserve?

_____
_____
_____
_____
_____
_____
_____
_____
_____
_____
_____

Day 306 - Are you treating yourself with the love and respect you
deserve?

_____
_____
_____
_____
_____
_____
_____
_____
_____
_____
_____

"The power of finding beauty in the humblest things
makes home happy and life lovely."
Louisa May Alcott

Day 307 - Write down at least five reasons why you're *enough.*

_____
_____
_____
_____
_____
_____
_____
_____
_____
_____
_____

Day 308 - When was the last time somebody told you *I love you?*

_____
_____
_____
_____
_____
_____
_____
_____
_____
_____
_____
_____

> "No act of kindness, no matter how small,
> is ever wasted."
> Aesop

Day 309 - When was the last time you told somebody *I love you*?

_____

Day 310 - When and why are you being sarcastic?

_____

> "Is time really moving on,
> or are you simply repeating patterns?"
> Zen Mirrors

Day 311 - Why do you *have to* improve yourself?

_____

_____

_____

_____

_____

_____

_____

_____

_____

_____

_____

Day 312 - Why are you a pleasant person to be around?

_____

_____

_____

_____

_____

_____

_____

_____

_____

_____

_____

"Great acts are made up of small deeds."
Lao Tzu

Day 313 - If you had $1 million dollars and you could only spend it on something that would improve the life of others, how would you spend it?

_____

_____

_____

_____

_____

_____

_____

_____

_____

_____

_____

_____

Day 314 - Do you enjoy being on your own? Why or why not?

_____

_____

_____

_____

_____

_____

_____

_____

_____

_____

_____

"We are the music makers, and we are the dreamers of dreams."
Arthur William Edgar O'Shaughnessy

Day 315 - How would you like to be remembered?

_____

_____

_____

_____

_____

_____

_____

_____

_____

_____

Day 316 - *Comfort zone ++++++++++*
Cook one totally new recipe this week. Write down what you are going
to cook and when you are going to do it.

_____

_____

_____

_____

_____

_____

_____

_____

_____

_____

"I had to deny knowledge in order to make room for faith."
Immanuel Kant

Day 317 - Who are the people that always believe in you?

Day 318 - What do you think about the most when you are alone?

"Love lights more fires than hate extinguishes."
Ella Wheeler Wilcox

Day 319 - Write down at least five things that make you feel genuinely positive about yourself.

_____
_____
_____
_____
_____
_____
_____
_____
_____

Day 320 - Do you believe that love can fade away? How does this relate to your own personal relationships?

_____
_____
_____
_____
_____
_____
_____
_____
_____
_____
_____

"It is never too late to be wise."
Daniel Defoe, *Robinson Crusoe*

Day 321 - What makes you fall out of love with someone?

Day 322 - What is something you do that would make people fall out of love with you?

"Everything that irritates us about others
can lead us to an understanding of ourselves."
Carl Gustav Jung

Day 323 - Where in your life are you too hard on other people?

_____

_____

_____

_____

_____

_____

_____

_____

_____

_____

Day 324 - What is the reason you would like to be famous?

_____

_____

_____

_____

_____

_____

_____

_____

_____

_____

_____

"I am sure there is Magic in everything, only we have not sense
enough to get hold of it and make it do things for us."
Frances Hodgson Burnett

Day 325 - Write down one paragraph to your partner or future partner,
so that he or she could understand you better. (it is an exercise you
don't actually *have to* give it to him or her)

_____

_____

_____

_____

_____

_____

_____

_____

_____

_____

_____

Day 326 - Is there meaning in suffering? Why or why not?

_____

_____

_____

_____

_____

_____

_____

_____

_____

_____

_____

"When one tugs at a single thing in nature,
he finds it attached to the rest of the world."
John Muir

Day 327 -How would you describe a healthy relationship?

_____

_____

_____

_____

_____

_____

_____

_____

_____

_____

_____

Day 328 -What aspect of other people makes you angry?

_____

_____

_____

_____

_____

_____

_____

_____

_____

_____

_____

_____

"If we do not find anything very pleasant,
at least we shall find something new."
Voltaire

Day 329 - What do you consider a sin? Why?

_____

_____

_____

_____

_____

_____

_____

_____

_____

Day 330 - What makes you afraid of getting older?

_____

_____

_____

_____

_____

_____

_____

_____

_____

_____

_____

"Romance is the glamour which turns the dust of everyday life into a golden haze."
Elinor Glyn

Day 331 - What does *home* mean to you?

_____

_____

_____

_____

_____

_____

_____

_____

_____

_____

_____

Day 332 - How would a perfect day look to you?

_____

_____

_____

_____

_____

_____

_____

_____

_____

_____

_____

"The first method for estimating the intelligence of a ruler
is to look at the men he has around him."
Niccolò Machiavelli

Day 333 - Do you feel like time is running out?

_____
_____
_____
_____
_____
_____
_____
_____
_____
_____

Day 334 - What is the one thing you could do today to make you
feel more self-confident?

_____
_____
_____
_____
_____
_____
_____
_____
_____
_____
_____

"Don't explain your philosophy. Embody it."
Epictetus

Day 335 - What is one thing you could do to connect more often with the most courageous, kindest and strongest version of yourself?

_____

_____

_____

_____

_____

_____

_____

_____

_____

_____

Day 336 - What would you like people to say to you more often?

_____

_____

_____

_____

_____

_____

_____

_____

_____

_____

"It may help us, in those times of trouble, to remember that love is not only about relationship, it is also an affair of the soul."
Thomas Moore

Day 337 - What dominating thoughts are running your life?

_____
_____
_____
_____
_____
_____
_____
_____
_____
_____
_____

Day 338 - Why does something have to be perfect?

_____
_____
_____
_____
_____
_____
_____
_____
_____
_____
_____
_____

"As she realized what might have been,
she grew to be thankful for what was."
Elizabeth Gaskell

Day 339 - Why does something have to be perfect?

_____
_____
_____
_____
_____
_____
_____
_____
_____
_____
_____

Day 340 - What about love scares you?

_____
_____
_____
_____
_____
_____
_____
_____
_____
_____
_____

"I am not proud, but I am happy; and happiness blinds,
I think, more than pride."

Alexandre Dumas, *The Count of Monte Cristo*

Day 341 - Are the deep desires you have actually scaring you? How?

_____

_____

_____

_____

_____

_____

_____

_____

_____

_____

Day 342 - What three things about the near future give you excitement?

_____

_____

_____

_____

_____

_____

_____

_____

_____

_____

"To put everything in balance is good,

to put everything in harmony is better."
Victor Hugo

Day 343 - If you were invited to write a one paragraph speech that would be broadcasted nationwide, how would it go?

_____

_____

_____

_____

_____

_____

_____

_____

_____

_____

Day 344 - Is it possible for people to change if they love someone?

_____

_____

_____

_____

_____

_____

_____

_____

_____

_____

_____

_____

> "It's the grown-up who disciplines himself,
> that can safely see the world as a child."
> Zen Mirrors

Day 345 - Could you change if you loved someone?

_____
_____
_____
_____
_____
_____
_____
_____
_____
_____

Day 346 - What makes you feel young and vibrant?

_____
_____
_____
_____
_____
_____
_____
_____
_____
_____

"A lie that is half-truth is the darkest of all lies."
Alfred Tennyson

Day 347 - What do you think is more important: progress or perfection? Why?

_____
_____
_____
_____
_____
_____
_____
_____
_____
_____

Day 348 - What do you think is more important progress or perfection and why?

_____
_____
_____
_____
_____
_____
_____
_____
_____
_____

> "Nothing is so painful to the human mind
> as a great and sudden change."
> Mary Wollstonecraft Shelley

Day 349 - What are three things that make you feel grateful about your life right now?

_____
_____
_____
_____
_____
_____
_____
_____
_____
_____
_____

Day 350 - How have you improved yourself over the last couple of months?

_____
_____
_____
_____
_____
_____
_____
_____
_____
_____
_____

"The Poetry of earth is never dead."

John Keats , English poet

Day 351 - *Comfort zone ++++++++++*
Go out in nature this week for at least 2.5 hours without any distraction. Preferably without a smartphone, but if you find it uncomfortable, bring your phone and put it on airplane mode. Afterwards, reflect on it. Write down when you are going to do it and when you are going to reflect on it.

_____

_____

_____

_____

_____

_____

_____

_____

_____

_____

Day 352 - If you died in two weeks, would what you worry about now still hold any significance? Why or why not?

_____

_____

_____

_____

_____

_____

_____

_____

"Being entirely honest with oneself is a good exercise."
Sigmund Freud

Day 353 - What do you and your partner have in common / name three things you would like you and your future partner to have in common?

_____

_____

_____

_____

_____

_____

_____

_____

_____

_____

_____

Day 354 - What particular lesson is life trying to teach you?

_____

_____

_____

_____

_____

_____

_____

_____

_____

_____

_____

_____

"Is time moving forward...
Or is it you who is running around in circles."
C.W. V. Straaten

Day 355 - What pain still needs to get out?

_____
_____
_____
_____
_____
_____
_____
_____
_____
_____
_____
_____

Day 356 - What do you find awkward about holding eye contact?

_____
_____
_____
_____
_____
_____
_____
_____
_____
_____
_____

"Busy with needing to speak, we missed the song."
Zen Mirrors

Day 357 - Imagine you met your 80-year old self tonight. What would he or she tell you not to worry about?

_____
_____
_____
_____
_____
_____
_____
_____
_____
_____
_____

Day 358 - Your 80-year old self decided to stay for the night. What would he or she say about your house?

_____
_____
_____
_____
_____
_____
_____
_____
_____
_____
_____

"Be to her virtues very kind,
Be to her faults a little blind."
Matthew Prior

Day 359 - Your 80-year old self decided to stay for one more night.
What is the one question you would ask him or her?
And what would be his or her answer?

_____

_____

_____

_____

_____

_____

_____

_____

_____

_____

Day 360 - If you stopped worrying about the future,
how would today be different?

_____

_____

_____

_____

_____

_____

_____

_____

_____

_____

Even if the sorrows stay,
new realizations will lighten your burden
and the burden of your fellow man.

Of future generations.
For no information ever goes wasted.
Then immerse yourself in something good
and together we will raise.

And we will say, yes, it is but a distant memory.
Chains will be gone.
And the rewards you will reap
Are not small in joy and inner wealth.

C.W. V. Straaten

Day 361 - What hidden tears hold the key to a new beginning?

"There is no such uncertainty as a sure thing."
Robert Burns

Day 362 - What song reminds you of good times?

_____
_____
_____
_____
_____
_____
_____
_____
_____
_____
_____

Day 363 - What would happen if you gave yourself the space
to be who you are?

_____
_____
_____
_____
_____
_____
_____
_____
_____
_____
_____
_____

"In silence, I hear my special song,
composed on the wings of this universe."
Zen Mirrors

Day 364 - What would happen if you acted as your most courageous
self when it comes to love?

_____

_____

_____

_____

_____

_____

_____

_____

_____

_____

_____

Day 365 - How could you live life to the fullest, at least for a moment?

_____

_____

_____

_____

_____

_____

_____

_____

_____

_____

_____

The end.

As an extra bonus, we provide a preview of the book *Win The Morning, Win The Day* by C.W. V. Straaten, also published by *True Potential Project.*

If you want to purchase this book you can find it on Amazon:

https://www.amazon.com/Win-Morning-Day-Life-Changing-Routine/dp/1723850543

Introduction

"Habit is a second nature, or rather,
it is 'ten times nature."

William James,
American philosopher and psychologist (1842 - 1910)

What would happen if every time you brushed your teeth or drove your car, it was as if you did it for the first time? It could be enjoyable for a couple of days to have constant new impressions. However, it would mean that a lot of your brainpower was already used before you even did your first important task of the day.

Habits help us to do things automatically so that we have the energy to think and work on more important things. In that sense, habits have enormous power over our life. You don't have to search too far on the internet (or your Facebook wall, or Instagram feed) to find wise quotes about the power of habits. Aristotle, Warren Buffett, Jim Rohn; they all understood that the key to success in life is far simpler than we might think. Choose the right habit and you're all set for success. The holy grail of self-development. Simple, right?

Simple yes, easy no!

This is not the first self-help book I have written. I am the author of two successful addiction recovery workbooks. In these books, I explain and give advice about the understanding of addiction and how to change this devastating condition. When you *demolish* the addiction, you see that it is actually a habit. A destructive and strong one, but nevertheless a habit. It could all start with one beer at dinner or buying your new running shoes on credit.

"Habits are powerful, but delicate. They can emerge outside our consciousness, or can be deliberately designed. They often occur without our permission, but can be reshaped by fiddling with their parts. They shape our lives far more than we realize—they are so strong, in fact, that they cause our brains to cling to them at the exclusion of all else, including common sense."

Charles Duhigg, *The Power Of Habit*

If habits have the power to become destructive addictions, the opposite is also true. Habits can massively change your life for the positive. So, what if you could take control of this magnificent force? What if you could create a constructive and empowering *keystone* habit that will develop a positive chain effect for almost every other area in life?

It is possible, and that's why I wrote this book. To give you the tools to create a simple but strong keystone habit to improve your life for good. This is not just textbook advice, or what I've seen in countless seminars, self-help talks and motivational speeches, or what I've read in hundreds of interviews with the best of the best such as Michael Phelps, Mel Robbins, and Michael Jordan: no, it's what I've experienced firsthand.

Since my gambling addiction a little over four years ago, my life has changed in ways you can't imagine. I am not going to boast here, but I went from broke, desperate and alone to a successful publisher and author, traveling the world and having the social life I want. Among a lot of other self-healing and self-improvement processes, the one thing that has changed my life the most is my morning ritual. My keystone habit. It's simple, peaceful and clear, and I am always doing it no matter what. It makes me *ready* for the day, ready for growth. It's true that small actions, repeated over time, have the tremendous power to change your life in astonishing ways.

Over the next pages, I will guide you to create your own morning ritual. A keystone habit that will change your life, if you follow through. To help you with that, this book is designed as a 21-day challenge. This will give you the chance to test this morning ritual concept for three weeks straight. If it isn't for you, after all, you've at least learned a new experience.

But, if it worked for you, you have set the first stage for creating a new and lasting habit.

Let this morning ritual be your force for a better life. Take the wheel. Decide what you want to do with your day. With as little as twenty to thirty minutes each day, you will create an empowering effect. Small steps lead to big changes.

Win The Morning, Win The Day!

Preparation

pre·pare prɪˈpɛː/
to make ready beforehand for a specific purpose;
to put in a proper state of mind;
created in advance; pre-planned

What is the one chance you'll get to take control of your life? That's right, your morning. Fortunately, that's a new chance every day. I could, and later will elaborate about the enormous scientifically-backed benefits of starting your day right. But more than name-dropping and citing interesting studies, let's get back to the one advisor that's always there for us (but seems to be shamelessly ignored most of the time) - common sense.

Compare the following; if you will run a marathon one year from now, what would be the ideal preparation?

1. Asking advice from other marathon runners, developing and starting a training scheme, buying the right shoes, consulting with a dietician, staying motivated for training by doing it together with a good friend and building a charity around your marathon goal.
2. Thinking about training and occasionally running a couple of miles throughout the year, and all of a sudden realizing, 'Oops...

Today is the day!'. Rushing out of bed and into your running shoes, going to the marathon and hoping for the best.

It's a simple, exaggerated example. But it isn't so far from the truth. How many big projects in your life do you start without decent preparation? It isn't about overthinking a situation for hours upon hours, it is about being *observant* of what you are about to do and asking yourself the right questions.

To put yourself in the right state of mind and to get ready.

This book is designed to do that. Create a crystal clear, healthy and energetic morning ritual that will serve you for the rest of your life. Begin your day motivated and well prepared, and belong to the few percent who do this. Getting ready for the day means getting ready for life.

How to use this book

This book is divided into two parts. The first part is where you are going to create your own morning ritual. This part has seven short chapters. Each chapter gives information, tips and guidelines to create a part of your morning ritual. For example, there is a part about power questions and a part about daily goal-setting (or intention setting). At the end of every chapter there are specific questions helping you to:

1. Start creating your own morning ritual
2. Take measures to follow through

When you have finished part 1 and created your morning ritual, it's time to start your 21-day challenge. In part 2 you will get the instructions needed for the challenge, including daily journaling questions.

The print version of this book is designed as a workbook. You can write down your morning ritual and other notes in the first part of this book, and/or in the extensive journal at the end of this book. There is also space (one page per day) to do the daily journaling exercises during the three-week challenge.

#1 *The First Step:*

Get Out Of Bed

"The next morning the alarm rang at 6 a.m. and the first thing I felt was dread. ... Then, I did something that I had never done before - I ignored how I felt. I didn't think I did what needed to be done."

Mel Robbins,
The 5 Second Rule

In a *Wall Street Journal* column titled *The Struggle to Wake Up Can Be Alarming,* behavioral scientist Dan Ariely writes about the negative effects of snoozing. He writes,

"In general, our bodies do better when they can get used to a single clear rule: Get out of bed the moment the alarm sounds. ... When we play with the snooze button, our bodies get a confused message: Sometimes we hear the beeping and get up, sometimes we hear it and stay put for 10 more minutes, ... So just bite the bullet and get out of bed when the alarm tells you to."

And he isn't the only one who dismantles one of the favorite morning rituals of hitting the snooze button.

Indeed, we could fill this chapter with scientists and professors who talk about the disadvantages of snoozing. From giving your body a cardiovascular assault to waking up even more groggy, it's not so hard to find the disadvantages of snoozing. But for us there is a way more important reason to get out of bed the moment your alarm goes off.

If you make a decision, have the courage to live up to it.

You set your alarm at night to wake up at a specific time in the morning. Snoozing means two things; procrastinating and not living up to your own agreements. If there is only one thing you take away from this workbook, it should be this: don't hit your snooze button ever again.

This habit alone could change your life.

Because this way, the first act of your day isn't one of procrastination. It isn't one of taking the easy, comfortable road: staying in bed. No, it is an act of courage and decisiveness.

creating A Morning Ritual #1

Pick a wake up time for the rest of these 21 Days and set the daily alarm. *(The time for your morning ritual should be at least 30 minutes, and preferably 45 minutes - 60 minutes)*

Not two, three or four alarms, just *one.* If you've made it this far in this book, you've already made the commitment to yourself to give the morning ritual a 21-day trial.

So, trust yourself with only one alarm. (Possibly you could use one alarm time for weekdays and a different alarm time for the weekend)

Try Mel Robbins' 5-seconds rule approach when you know that *no snoozing* is going to be difficult. It's a rule where you count backward from 5 to 1 and then **act**. In this case, getting out of bed. I highly recommend Robbins' book, *The 5-Second Rule*. For a quick introduction to the rule, watch her TED talk here: https://www.youtube.com/watch?v=Lp7E973zozc.

Your Morning Ritual #1

My alarm time for weekdays is going to be:

_____

My alarm time for the weekend is going to be:

_____

This is what I am going to do, to prevent myself from using the snooze button and to makes sure that I'll get out of bed:

End of the preview. If you want to purchase this journal you can find it on Amazon.

About *21 Exercises*

We specialize in creating empowering, elegant & inspirational self-help journals. The power of journaling, of consistent self-reflection, is a scientifically proven habit that will benefit your life in truly astonishing ways. Mainly 90-Day or Yearly Journals, on various topics and for all types of people. Tools for self-reflection, gratitude & personal growth. We create each journal or workbook with the utmost care and the honest intention to give lasting benefit to our customers.

We hope to guide you through releasing limitations and discover your hidden potentials in all areas of life. And of course to give an enjoyable journaling experience. Step by step, to unlock the true you. Step by step, to a better world.

We'd love to hear your ideas, tips, and questions. Let us know at exercises21@yahoo.com

The 365 Self-Discovery Journal

Made in United States
North Haven, CT
14 September 2023

41555198R00125